A BEACON BIOGRAPHY

Ellen DeGeneres

Tamra B. Orr

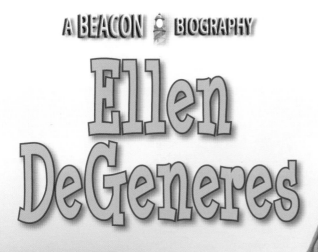

PURPLE TOAD
PUBLISHING

PURPLE TOAD
PUBLISHING

Printing   1   2   3   4   5   6   7   8   9

A Beacon Biography

Angelina Jolie
Big Time Rush
Cam Newton
Carly Rae Jepsen
Daisy Ridley
Drake
Ed Sheeran
Ellen DeGeneres
Elon Musk
Harry Styles of One Direction
Jennifer Lawrence
John Boyega
Kevin Durant
Lorde
Malala
Maria von Trapp
Markus "Notch" Persson, Creator of Minecraft
Mo'ne Davis
Muhammad Ali
Neil deGrasse Tyson
Peyton Manning
Robert Griffin III (RG3)

Publisher's Cataloging-in-Publication Data
Orr, Tamra.
    Ellen DeGeneres / written by Tamra Orr.
        p. cm.
Includes bibliographic references, glossary, and index.
ISBN 9781624692543
1. DeGeneres, Ellen—Juvenile literature. 2. Comedians—United States--Biography—Juvenile literature. 3. Television personalities—United States—Biography—Juvenile literature. I. Series: Beacon biography.
    PN2287.D358 2017
    792.702

Library of Congress Control Number: 2016936350

eBook ISBN: 9781624692550

ABOUT THE AUTHOR: Tamra B. Orr is a full-time author living in the Pacific Northwest. She has written more than 450 educational books for readers of all ages. She is a graduate of Ball State University and commonly gives presentations to schools and conferences. She admits to watching *The Ellen DeGeneres Show* for years and often finds herself in tears—either from laughter or from Ellen's touching acts of kindness.

PUBLISHER'S NOTE: This story has not been authorized or endorsed by Ellen DeGeneres.

CONTENTS

As usual, Ellen's speech when accepting her Humanitarian award had her unique blend of humor and honesty.

"A Human and an 'Itarian"

The Microsoft Theater in Los Angeles, California, is used to hosting award shows, with famous celebrities and loud applause. For years, it was known as the Nokia Theatre L.A. Live. It has been home to a wide range of exciting events, from the annual Emmy Awards to several seasons of the television show *American Idol.* Thousands of people fill the seats, ready to cheer and clap as contestants and winners stroll onto the stage.

On the evening of January 7, 2016, the theater exploded with applause. In seconds, all of the celebrities were on their feet, yelling and shouting in support of one of their own: Ellen DeGeneres. After a heartfelt introduction by actor Melissa McCarthy, DeGeneres was presented with the 2016 People's Choice Favorite Humanitarian Award. This award is not given lightly. To qualify, a person must have "dedicated his or her time to fighting indifference, intolerance, and injustice." Past winners have included actor Sandra Bullock and singer Jennifer Hudson.

As usual, as she accepted the award, DeGeneres was both funny and kind. "This is crazy. I mean, so, so deserved, but this is crazy," she said, with a smile. "I have to say, it's a little strange to actually get an award for being nice and generous and kind, which is what we're all supposed to do with one another. That's the point of being a human." She added that the award must have been designed for her, as it "sums me up perfectly, as I am both a

A hallmark of Ellen's talk show is the kindness and generosity she shows to a variety of guests. Here she donates $50,000 to a family that lost their home and had to sell all of their possessions.

human and an *'itarian*."[1] The award came with $200,000, which DeGeneres donated directly to St. Jude Children's Research Hospital.

Being funny has been what made actor and talk show host Ellen DeGeneres famous. However, it has been her unlimited compassion and kindness for other people that have turned her into one of the most beloved celebrities in the world. "The most important thing for me is to know that I represent kindness," DeGeneres said in an interview with *Good Housekeeping*. "I'm glad I'm funny. I'm glad I make people happy, because that's very important. But I'm proud to be known as a kind person."[2]

DeGeneres believes that the unkind and sarcastic humor in the world often leads to issues like bullying. "It's nasty," she continued in the same interview. "Kids grow up hearing that, and they think that's what humor is, and they think it's OK. But that negativity permeates the entire planet … .

So, I'm really proud I'm not adding to the negativity. I'm proud that for the hour my show is on television, I'm not being mean, and I'm hopefully helping one other person go, *I'm going to be kind.* Because then it all just kind of spreads, and the world is a little nicer out there."[3]

When DeGeneres was quite young, she had already decided what she wanted to do with her life. "I wanted to have money, I wanted to be special, I wanted people to like me," she admitted. "I wanted to be famous." When she was standing onstage, holding the Humanitarian Award and being cheered by thousands of her fans in the theater—and millions more watching from home—it was clear that DeGeneres had accomplished every one of those goals.[4]

Ellen is known for her silly side. She and Carrie Fisher, the actor who played Princess Leia in the Star Wars movies, wear Princess Leia hair buns to sell movie tickets for charity.

NEW ORLEANS

METAIRIE

Ellen adored her older brother and often wanted to be just like him.

Ellen grew up in the busy business district of Metairie in New Orleans.

Coping with Changes

The woman who would one day be rich, popular, famous, and special was born on January 26, 1958, in Metairie, a suburb of New Orleans. Ellen Lee DeGeneres' mother, Betty, was a real estate agent, and her father, Elliot, was an insurance salesman. Already waiting at home was Ellen's three-and-a-half-year-old brother, Vance. For years, Vance was Ellen's role model. "When you're growing up and you see your brother, who's talented and gorgeous and all these things, you want to be all those things," she said to *W Magazine*. "I was always observant," she added.[1]

Unfortunately, not everything Ellen saw was pleasant. "I noticed that my brother got lots of attention and that my parents didn't have a good marriage," she admitted in the same interview. "I always wanted to shake things up."[2]

When she was in elementary school, Ellen thought about becoming a veterinarian. She loved animals of all kinds—a love that has continued throughout her life—but did not think she was smart enough to become a vet. Instead, after graduating from Texas' Atlanta High School in 1976, she headed off to the University of New Orleans to study communication. She quit after a single semester.

During those years, the future comedian had all kinds of jobs. She waited tables at TGI Fridays and shucked oysters in New Orleans' French Quarter.

Making people smile was one of Ellen's best defenses.

She also bartended, painted houses, and demonstrated vacuums in front of store customers.

Life at home was tough for DeGeneres. Her family had moved often, and Ellen felt as if she were always the new kid at school. Her mother says Ellen used humor as her icebreaker when meeting new students. It was hard to keep adjusting, though.

"We never owned a house when I was growing up," Ellen said in the *Good Housekeeping* interview. "We rented, and we moved about every two years, just far enough to have to start a new school. Also, my mother was a real estate agent for a little while, so I was always looking at houses with her. We couldn't afford to buy one, so it was a frustrating thing as a kid. You're imagining, *This is going to be my room*, and then it was like, 'Oh, we can't afford it.' Well, why are we looking at it?"[3]

When she was a young teenager, her parents divorced. Vance decided to live with their father. "When my parents divorced, it was my mother and me, by ourselves in an apartment," Ellen said. "At that point, we kind of became roommates. I was thirteen years old. She'd been married for almost twenty years, and I watched her go through a tough time, trying to date, trying to figure things out," Ellen recalled in the *Good Housekeeping* interview. "So, at thirteen, I kind of became an adult and was taking care of . . . watching her struggle. It made me go, *Oh, you're my mom, but you're also just a human being.* I saw her in a different role all of a sudden."[4]

One of the adult roles DeGeneres had to take on was protecting her mother from bad dating choices. "She dated some horrible men," Ellen told

Good Housekeeping, "whom I had to kick out of the house. ... Certainly, she [Betty] has persevered. My mom had some really bad things happen in her life, and she's a trouper. She's tougher than I am, I'd say."[5]

When Ellen was sixteen years old, Betty married a salesman named Roy Gruessendorf. The family moved from New Orleans to Atlanta, Texas. Years later, as an adult, Ellen revealed that her stepfather molested her on several occasions. She found herself locking her bedroom door, and once, she even had to "kick out a window and escape and sleep in a hospital all night long," *CBS News* reported.[6] Ellen decided to share her story because "it's important for teenage girls out there to hear that there are different ways to say no. And if it ever happens to them, they should tell someone right away."[7]

Ellen's sense of humor kept her going when life was tough. Little did she know that that same sense of humor would lead her to everything she had ever hoped to have.

Ellen and her mother continue to be best friends.

> In the beginning, it was just Ellen, the stage, a microphone, and a hope to make people laugh.

"Soup of the Day"

By the early 1980s, DeGeneres knew she was funny—but how could she turn that into a career? She decided to try doing stand-up comedy and began appearing in local coffeehouses. Slowly, she started to branch out to other states, and then she began traveling across the country, appearing in small bars and clubs.

In 1982, she took one of her best routines and submitted it to the cable channel Showtime. She won the title of Funniest Person in Louisiana. She went on to compete and win the national title: Showtime's Funniest Person in America. Meanwhile, she was also working as the emcee of Clyde's Comedy Club in New Orleans.

It wasn't easy making people laugh. "You have to be really, really tough-skinned," she told *W Magazine*. "There's lots of traveling, lots of being by yourself, lots of really rude, drunk people. You're not just in big cities," she continued, "you're in small towns, mini malls, strip malls . . . lots of places where, literally, the soup of the day got top billing. There would be a chalkboard on the sidewalk and it would say, 'SOUP OF THE DAY: Broccoli and Ellen DeGeneres.' "[1]

Her style of humor was getting noticed, however. One day, she caught the attention of one of the most important people in show business: Johnny Carson. As the longtime host of *The Tonight Show*, before the days of Jay

Johnny Carson hosted The Tonight Show *for 30 years. An appearance on his show could change a person's life overnight.*

Leno and Jimmy Fallon, Carson often brought new musicians and comedians onto his show. Those who did well often had a real chance at stardom. Usually, the new performers appeared for mere moments, and when their song or routine was finished, they took a bow and disappeared behind the show's curtain. If Johnny called them over to sit down for a moment and chat, however, success was almost guaranteed.

When DeGeneres appeared on *The Tonight Show* on November 28, 1986,

Ellen's comedy was a huge hit with the audience—and with Carson.

she was nervous. At 27, this was her first appearance on network television. She came out on stage and performed for several moments, including her now famous routine, "A Phone Call with God." When she was done, Johnny called her over to sit down.

Ellen did a good job of not appearing as nervous as she was when talking to the legendary talk show host.

"The fact that he wanted me to sit down and talk to him, it catapulted my career," she told *The Guardian*. "[But] that's not why I wanted to do it. I wanted to do it because I knew he would appreciate it. I knew it was smart, I knew it was different, and I knew that nobody was doing what I was doing. That's all I wanted, I wanted people to *get me*."[2]

After Carson's show, Ellen became a familiar face on talk shows. She would no longer be billed next to the day's soup.

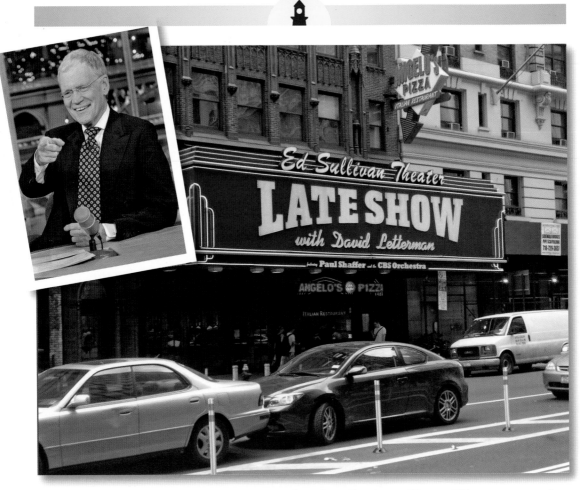

During David Letterman's many years hosting The Late Show, Ellen appeared multiple times.

Following her appearance on *The Tonight Show*, DeGeneres' career took off. She began appearing regularly on talk shows such as *The Late Show with David Letterman*, *The Oprah Winfrey Show*, *Larry King Live* and *Good Morning, America*. It was not long before she began appearing on television sitcoms. She had a small role as a peppy receptionist at a real estate firm on *Open House*. As DeGeneres described her character, "She was so over the top and so weird!"[3] DeGeneres also had a role in the show *Laurie Hill* in 1992.

It was in 1994 that DeGeneres found stardom. She was given her own television series. Originally called *These Friends of Mine*, the title was changed to *Ellen*. She played Ellen Morgan, a bookstore employee. It was a huge hit and won many awards. She also published her first book in 1995, titled, *My Point . . . and I Do Have One*. People loved her style, and she was asked to host the Grammys in 1996 and 1997.

But a big change was ahead. As successful as she was, DeGeneres was keeping a secret from the rest of the world, and it was one she was about to share.

These *Friends of Mine* cast (from left): Joely Fisher, Jeremy Piven, Ellen DeGeneres, Arye Gross, David Anthony Higgins, Clea Lewis

TIME

Yep,
I'm Gay

EXCLUSIVE: Ellen
DeGeneres explains
why she's coming out

The changing
nature of sex on TV

"Yep, I'm Gay"

Just as she was becoming known across the world, Ellen took a brave step. It was one that indirectly helped many people throughout the world.

One day in 1977, DeGeneres took a long walk with her mother and confessed that she was in love. Naturally, her mother was excited. Then Ellen told Betty she was in love with another woman. "I was taken by surprise," Betty admitted. "I didn't know what it meant. I realized she would suddenly be an object of derogatory remarks, and I loved her too much for that."[1]

It would be another twenty years before Ellen would share this secret with the rest of the world. By then, she had starred in the movie *Mr. Wrong* and was doing well with her sitcom. It was exhausting pretending to be someone she wasn't. "It was scary and crazy," she told *Us Weekly* magazine. She wondered if people would "still love me if they knew I was gay? And my fear was that no, no they wouldn't, and then it made me feel ashamed that I was hiding something. It made me feel ashamed that I couldn't feel honest and really be who I am, and I just didn't want to pretend to be somebody else anymore so that people would like me."[2]

DeGeneres finally decided to announce that she was gay. First, she appeared on the cover of the April 14, 1997, issue of *Time*, along with the headline, "Yep, I'm Gay." She was the country's first openly gay female celebrity. Two weeks later, "The Puppy Episode" of her television show aired to 42 million viewers. On this famous episode, after meeting another gay

In 1997, Ellen won an Emmy for the acclaimed "Puppy Episode." As happy as she was, it came at a cost.

character, played by actor Laura Dern, Ellen Morgan announces she is a lesbian.

There were many different reactions to DeGeneres' announcement. Gay support groups across the country applauded her honesty. She also received a great deal of criticism. Even though she had won an Emmy for the show, some of her sponsors yanked their commercials in protest.

"Even though I had a big foundation with my career and years of work, it just divided everyone when I came out," DeGeneres told *Good Housekeeping*. "Simply my saying I was gay—even though I was the exact same person—divided everyone. People stopped watching the show, so some advertisers pulled out. It didn't matter that I was a good, devoted, loyal employee. I mean, I showed up on time. I never did anything wrong. I was kind. I was easy to work with. And yet it was the dollar that mattered more."[3]

In 1998, *Ellen* was canceled.

The next three years were tough for DeGeneres. She spent a great deal of time battling depression. "It was just a huge dose of reality for me. But losing it all really gave me time to realize that all this stuff is very fleeting," she revealed. "If success is really dependent on someone liking you or not liking you, and you have to teeter on that tightrope of how you're supposed to act and how you're supposed to look and who you are, it's just not a healthy way to live."[4]

In 1999, DeGeneres had roles in the movies *EDtv* and *The Love Letter*. In 2000, she appeared in the television show *If These Walls Could Talk 2*. She even tried to have her own show again on CBS. Called *The Ellen Show*, it was quickly canceled. During those years, she dated other actors, including Anne Heche and Alexandra Hedison.

Although Ellen dealt with people who did not understand or accept her sexuality, she also became a spokesperson and role model for the gay community.

In November 2001, the country was still reeling from the September 11 attacks in New York and Washington, D.C. DeGeneres was asked to host the annual Emmy awards, and she did it with style and grace. Making people laugh at such an emotional time was not easy. During the show, she stated, "I felt it was important for me to be here tonight, because what would bug the Taliban more than seeing a gay woman in a suit surrounded by Jews?"[5]

Hosting an awards show when the country was in mourning was no small challenge. Ellen managed to do so, helping people laugh and heal.

At the end of the show, DeGeneres was given a standing ovation. She hosted the awards show again in 2005, as well the Academy Awards in 2007 and 2014. She was only the second woman in Academy history to act as host (the first was Whoopi Goldberg). At the 2014 Academy Awards she took a selfie with a dozen other celebrities that was re-tweeted so many times, it temporarily shut down Twitter. She also ordered pizza for everyone in the audience.

Life was finally turning around. DeGeneres wanted to find just the right type of show that she would enjoy and would showcase her strongest talents—being funny and kind. In 2003, she found the perfect place.

In one of the world's most famous selfies, Ellen gathered celebrities Jared Leto, Jennifer Lawrence, Meryl Streep, Julia Roberts, Kevin Spacey, Brad Pitt, Bradley Cooper, Lupita Nyong'o and Nyong'o's brother Peter, and Angelina Jolie.

Ellen's talk show has remained a favorite since it started in 2003. It continues to win awards and entertain millions of viewers every day.

The Spectrum of Happiness

Anyone who tunes in to a daily episode of *The Ellen DeGeneres Show* can see that DeGeneres is a happy woman. From her energetic dance moves to the big smile on her face, she glows. The last few years have seen her happier than she ever thought she could be—and she shares her good fortune with as many people as she can. "I want the show to reach people and to be something positive," DeGeneres told *W Magazine*. "[In 1998] I lost my show, I lost my entire career, and I lost everything for three years." She added that she was lucky to get another chance. "I got to learn I was strong enough to start over again."[1]

When DeGeneres' daytime talk show began in 2003, it was a huge hit. It won 15 Emmy Awards in its first three years. By 2014, the show had earned 25. DeGeneres has become known as the Queen of Daytime. On each show, she has made sure to report uplifting stories, to bring on celebrity guests as well as talented kids, and to inspire people. She gives away millions of dollars in products and money to those who need them. She is actively involved in many different charities, which are listed and described on her web site, Ellen's Organizations.

As an animal lover, she is also very active in the Humane Society and the Gentle Barn. In 2009, PETA (People for the Ethical Treatment of Animals) named her Woman of the Year. Two years later, DeGeneres became a vegan.

Dory

She also became known to children all over the world when she provided the voice of the forgetful fish Dory in Disney's 2003 movie *Finding Nemo.* She would do the same thing for the sequel, *Finding Dory,* in 2016. In 2011, her second book, *Seriously . . . I'm Kidding,* was published.

Along with her extremely popular television show, DeGeneres has found happiness in another area. In December 2004, she met actor Portia de Rossi. On August 16, 2008, during the period when California allowed same-sex marriage, the two were married.

"Getting married was more important to her, really," DeGeneres said about de Rossi in *O: The Oprah Magazine.* "She says all the time how lucky we are that we had each other in that short window of time when it was legal to marry, because a lot of people hadn't found their person, and then suddenly that right was taken away. I'm tearing up thinking about it," she admitted. "We got to be *married,* and have a wedding. I grew up thinking I'd never get to do that."[2]

In 2009, DeGeneres was asked to be the face of Covergirl cosmetics. The following year, she was asked to be a judge on the popular competition show *American Idol.* She was happy to do so—but it was not a good fit for her. She loved being able to encourage people, not judge them. "I also realized this season that while I love discovering,

Ellen with President Barack Obama

supporting, and nurturing young talent, it was hard for me to judge people and sometimes hurt their feelings," she told the *LA Times*.[3]

Young DeGeneres would probably never have been able to imagine the success she would one day reach. "It's amazing to me that I have achieved what I've achieved," she told *NBC News*. "Nothing has been easy. Not one step of the way has been easy. I'm really proud that I'm strong, because I didn't think I was strong. And I think that when you bring up Dory, you know, there's that moment in the movie when [Marlin's] saying . . . goodbye to her.

Ellen and Portia have been called one of Hollywood's happiest couples.

And she starts crying and says, *I feel like I'm home.* That's what I feel like. I feel like I am finally home with everything."[4]

In an interview with *Good Housekeeping*, she added, "I'm definitely happier than I've ever been. I assume tomorrow I'll be happier than today, because things are great. I have a great career and I have wonderful fans who really are supportive and loyal—because I'm not hiding anything from them. So, on the spectrum of happiness, I'm pretty high up there."[5]

Ellen DeGeneres wanted to be famous and loved, and she has become both. She helps remind people that caring about each other is the key to anyone's success. "I think we need more love in the world," she told *Good Housekeeping* in 2011. "We need more kindness, more compassion, more joy, more laughter. I definitely want to contribute to that. I really want my time here to be positive and productive."[6]

1958 Ellen Lee DeGeneres is born in Metairie, Louisiana, on January 26.

1976 She graduates from Atlanta High School in Texas. After one semester at the University of New Orleans, she decides to drop out of college.

1982 She is named Showtime's Funniest Person in America.

1986 She appears on *The Tonight Show Starring Johnny Carson*.

1989 She has a small role (Margo Van Meter) on the TV show *Open House*.

1992 She plays Nancy McIntyre in the TV show *Laurie Hill*.

1994 She lands her own TV sitcom called *The Ellen Show*.

1995 Her book, *My Point . . . and I Do Have One*, is published.

1997 Ellen comes out as gay in both *Time* magazine and in her sitcom.

1998 *The Ellen Show* is canceled.

1999 DeGeneres appears in the movies *EDtv* and *The Love Letter*.

2001 Shortly after the terrorist attacks on September 11, she hosts the Emmy Awards with grace.

2003 She begins hosting a daytime talk show called *The Ellen DeGeneres Show*. She is the voice actor for Dory in *Finding Nemo*.

2008 She marries Portia de Rossi while it is legal to do so in California.

2009 People for the Ethical Treatment of Animals (PETA) names her Woman of the Year. Ellen becomes the face of Covergirl cosmetics.

2010 She has a short stint as a judge on *American Idol*.

2011 She becomes a vegan. Her second book, *Seriously . . . I'm Kidding*, is published.

2012 She becomes a spokesperson for JCPenney stores. She begins working as a producer for the television show *Bethenny*.

2014 She hosts the Academy Awards show.

2015 She begins directing the sitcom *One Big Happy*.

2016 She is given the People's Choice Award for Favorite Humanitarian. She again is the voice of Dory in Disney/Pixar's *Finding Dory*.

Chapter 1

1. Naja Rayne, "Watch Ellen DeGeneres Be Hilarious Yet Touching Accepting the People's Choice Award for Favorite Humanitarian," *People*, January 7, 2016.

2. David Hochman, "Ellen DeGeneres: Nice Girls Finish First," *Good Housekeeping*, September 10, 2011.

3. Ibid.

4. Ben Walters, "Ellen DeGeneres: The Oscars Host Who Came Out of the Cold," *The Guardian*, March 1, 2014.

Chapter 2

1. Bridget Foley, "Ellen DeGeneres," *W Magazine*, March 2007.

2. Ibid.

3. David Hochman, "Ellen DeGeneres: Nice Girls Finish First," *Good Housekeeping*, September 10, 2011.

4. Ibid.

5. Ibid.

6. Bootie Cosgrove-Mather, "Ellen DeGeneres Molested as Teen," *CBS News*, May 18, 2005.

7. Hochman.

Chapter 3

1. Bridget Foley, "Ellen DeGeneres," *W Magazine*, March 2007.

2. Ben Walters, "Ellen DeGeneres: The Oscars Host Who Came Out of the Cold," *The Guardian*, March 1, 2014.

3. Naja Rayne, "Watch Ellen DeGeneres Be Hilarious Yet Touching Accepting the People's Choice Award for Favorite Humanitarian," *People*, January 7, 2016.

Chapter 4

1. "Ellen DeGeneres: Early Years," *Biography*.

2. Joyce Chen, "Ellen DeGeneres on Coming Out as Gay: 'I Didn't Think I Was Going to Come Out, Period,'" *Us Magazine*, October 23, 2015.

3. David Hochman, "Ellen DeGeneres: Nice Girls Finish First," *Good Housekeeping*, September 10, 2011.

4. Ibid.

5. Megan Riedlinger, "Ellen DeGeneres' Life in Pictures," *Wonderwall*, January 25, 2016.

Chapter 5

1. "Celebrity Central: Ellen DeGeneres," *People*, undated.

2. Oprah Winfrey, "Oprah Talks to Ellen DeGeneres," *O: The Oprah Magazine*, December 2009.

3. Scott Collins. "Ellen DeGeneres Is Out as American Idol Judge," *Los Angeles Times*, July 29, 2010.

4. Stone Phillips, "Catching Up with Ellen DeGeneres," *Dateline NBC*, November 8, 2004.

5. David Hochman, "Ellen DeGeneres: Nice Girls Finish First," *Good Housekeeping*, September 10, 2011.

6. Ibid.

Books

Cooke, CW. *Female Force: Women of the Media: A Graphic Novel: Oprah, Barbara Walters, Ellen DeGeneres and Meredith Vieira.* Vancouver, WA: Bluewater Productions, 2010.

Paprocki, Sherry. *Ellen DeGeneres: Entertainer.* Haverford, PA: Chelsea House Publishing, 2008.

Pohlen, Jerome. *Gay & Lesbian History for Kids: The Century-Long Struggle for LGBT Rights, with 21 Activities.* Chicago: Chicago Review Press, 2015.

Ruckdeschel, Sandra C. *Female Force: Ellen DeGeneres.* Portland, OR: Stormfront Entertainment, 2015.

Seba, Jaime. *Ellen DeGeneres: From Comedy Club to Talk Show.* Broomall, PA: Mason Crest, 2014.

Sharp, Katie. *Ellen DeGeneres (People in the News).* San Diego, CA: Lucent Books, 2010.

York, M.J. *12 Entertainers Who Changed the World.* Mankato, MN: 12-Story Library, 2015.

Web Sites

"The Ellen DeGeneres Show"—Kid Clips
> http://www.ellentv.com/kids/
> http://www.ellentv.com/tags/TalentedKids/

Ellen's Charity Organizations
> http://www.ellentv.com/tags/EllensOrganizations/

"Heads Up!"—The Game
> http://www.ellentv.com/2013/05/02/download-ellens-app-heads-up/

Works Consulted

"Celebrity Central: Ellen DeGeneres." *People.* Undated. http://www.people.com/people/ellen_DeGeneres/biography

Chen, Joyce. "Ellen DeGeneres on Coming Out as Gay: 'I Didn't Think I Was Going to Come Out, Period.' *Us Magazine.* October 23, 2015. http://www.usmagazine.com/celebrity-news/news/ellen-DeGeneres-on-coming-out-as-gay-i-didnt-think-i-was-going-to-20152310

Collins, Scott. "Ellen DeGeneres Is Out as 'American Idol' Judge." *Los Angeles Times.* July 29, 2010. http://articles.latimes.com/2010/jul/29/entertainment/la-et-ellen-DeGeneres-american-idol

Cosgrove-Mather, Bootie. "Ellen DeGeneres Molested as Teen." *CBS News.* May 18, 2005. http://www.cbsnews.com/news/ellen-DeGeneres-molested-as-teen/

"Ellen DeGeneres: Early Years." *Biography.* http://www.biography.com/people/ellen-degeneres-9542420/videos/ellen-degeneres-early-years-20723779715

Foley, Bridget. "Ellen DeGeneres." *W Magazine.* March 2007. http://www.wmagazine.com/people/celebrities/2007/03/ellen_DeGeneres/

Hochman, David. "Ellen DeGeneres' Nice Girls Finish First." *Good Housekeeping,* September 10, 2011. http://www.goodhousekeeping.com/life/inspirational-stories/interviews/a18893/ellen-DeGeneres-interview/

Phillips, Stone. "Catching Up with Ellen DeGeneres." *Dateline NBC,* November 8, 2004. http://www.nbcnews.com/id/6430100/ns/dateline_nbc-newsmakers/t/catching-ellen-DeGeneres-/#.VqmLm_krLhd

Rayne, Naja. "Watch Ellen DeGeneres Be Hilarious Yet Touching Accepting the People's Choice Award for Favorite Humanitarian." *People,* January 7, 2016. http://www.people.com/article/ellen-DeGeneres-hilariously-accepts-humanitarian-award-peoples-choice-awards

Riedlinger, Megan. "Ellen DeGeneres' Life in Pictures," *Wonderwall,* January 25, 2016, http://www.wonderwall.com/celebrity/profiles/ellen-degeneres-life-in-pictures-33511.gallery?photoId=167883.

Walters, Ben. "Ellen DeGeneres: The Oscars Host Who Came Out of the Cold." *The Guardian,* March 1, 2014. http://www.theguardian.com/film/2014/mar/01/ellen-DeGeneres-us-talkshow-host

Winfrey, Oprah. "Oprah Talks to Ellen DeGeneres." *O: The Oprah Magazine,* December 2009. http://www.oprah.com/omagazine/Oprah-Interviews-Ellen-DeGeneres-Ellens-O-Magazine-Cover

FILMOGRAPHY

2016	*Finding Dory*
2014	*Unity*
2004	*My Short Film*
2003	*Pauly Shore Is Dead*
	Exploring the Reef
	Finding Nemo
2000	*If These Walls Could Talk 2*
1999	*The Love Letter*

1999	*EDtv*
1998	*Dr. Doolittle*
	Goodbye Lover
1996	*Mr. Wrong*
1994	*Trevor*
1993	*Coneheads*
1991	*Wisecracks*
1990	*Arduous Moon*

GLOSSARY

catapult (KAT-uh-pult)—To launch dramatically.

contestant (kun-TES-tunt)—A person who takes part in a contest.

derogatory (duh-RAH-guh-tor-ee)—Insulting or unkind.

emcee (em-SEE)—Master of ceremonies, host.

molested (moh-LES-ted)—Sexually abused.

observant (ub-ZER-vunt)—Paying strict attention; noticing everything.

ovation (oh-VAY-shun)—Long and loud applause.

permeate (PER-mee-ayt)—To spread through.

semester (seh-MES-ter)—The first or second half of a school year.

shuck (SHUK)—To split and remove the outer shell of a clam or oyster.

spectrum (SPEK-trum)—The whole range of a set of values.

Taliban (TAL-ih-ban)—The terrorist group behind the September 11, 2001, attacks on the United States. The Taliban have many prejudices, including a hatred for Jewish people and a belief that women are inferior to men.

vegan (VEE-gun)—A person who does not eat or use any kind of animal products, including eggs, dairy, and leather.

veterinarian (veh-treh-NAYR-ee-un)—A doctor who takes care of animals.